The Adventures of a School Volunteer: Karl's Here!

by Karl Van Asselt

ABOUT THE BOOK

Karl's Here! is a unique look at elementary school volunteering. The author's personal account of his volunteer experiences provides a look at the interaction between the volunteer, the teacher, and the students. Karl's volunteer roles are detailed as he becomes part of the classroom teaching team. He describes volunteer-led "Special and Fun Projects" with the students that are woven into the class curriculum by the teacher. Karl argues that adults, particularly senior citizens, can make a significant impact in the classroom, have fun, and receive a host of unexpected personal rewards.

ABOUT THE AUTHOR

Karl Van Asselt has authored six books, published more than 60 articles in journals and magazines, and has been engaged in newspaper writing for decades. Now semi-retired, Karl elected to spend some of his free time as an elementary school volunteer. "I had no intention of writing about the volunteer experience," Karl says. "But I had repeatedly told the students that they would enjoy writing if they wrote about fun, personal experiences. I decided to follow my own good advice and write about my school experience."

CONTENTS

ACKNOWLEDGMENTS

Thanks to "my" teachers, Ms. Canner and Ms. Cowan, who took a chance and gave me an opportunity to volunteer. After all, if it didn't work, they had to fix it. Thanks to Ms. Maxfield, the Barrington Elementary School Principal, for the book's "Introduction" and for looking the other way when I arrived at school. Thanks to Marge, Jessica, Cathy, Cheryl and others who, by listening to my "school stories," inadvertently encouraged me to write this book. Thanks to Jessica who packaged it up and made the words fit. Thanks to my friend Rachel for her wonderful editing, an art she has promised to someday teach me. And a very special thanks to the very special 35 third and fourth graders who made my volunteer experience so very rewarding.

INTRODUCTION

Volunteers in Our Schools

by Mary Maxfield, Principal, Barrington (NH) Elementary School

Volunteering in our public schools has been a long-standing, all-American, do-good kind of idea. In the late 60s and 70s, I remember the well-dressed, "good smelling" moms arriving at school just after the morning bell rang or sometimes just for an afternoon. They would duplicate worksheets using the purple smudged mimeograph machine, and the really nice ones let us smell the damp fluid-laced pages as they cranked them out. Sometimes these wonderful volunteers supervised recess activities, holiday parties, and helped with projects. They always had a smile, they were always sweet, and they were always women.

Times have changed. Our schools have changed. But the need for volunteers is greater than ever. While assistance with copying, filing, and laminating still exists, volunteers can do much more to enrich our students' learning experiences. And I am quite sure most folks, particularly our senior population, sell themselves short in terms of what they have to offer our school children of today.

In Karl's first year of volunteering, he challenged a group of third grade students to write about five, and only five, things that matter to them in their lives. Through weeks of processing, discussions, writing and editing, students made their decisions and wrote beautifully about their "Five Things That Matter."

Karl makes kids think. And while I prefer to be razzing Karl whenever the opportunity arises, alas, I must give credit where credit is due and admit that Karl makes me think, too. As I approached this task of writing about the value of volunteers in our schools, I challenged myself, à la Karl, to choose five things that matter for our students, and the impact volunteers can truly have on those five things.

> 1. **Challenge.** *We need to provide an education for children that is challenging.* Volunteers, particularly older, more seasoned volunteers, provide students with a lifetime of vocabulary and questions that make students think.

Students respond by explaining their thinking, supporting their opinions, and arguing their point of view. Our students often think deeply and express themselves more fully when working with a volunteer. They *want* to make the volunteer understand them and their work. Volunteers can challenge our students.

2.   **Engagement.** *We need to provide an education for children that is engaging.* Giving our students attention and opportunity for interactions increases their engagement. Students working in a small group with a volunteer are given the opportunity and the time to ask questions, seek clarification and perspective, and to receive help moving forward with a task or assignment. Volunteers help keep our students engaged.

3.   **Relevance.** *We need to provide an education for children that is relevant.* "How am I ever going to use this?" is a question still being asked by students, and volunteers with life experiences can truly answer those questions. We live in the "just Google it" world, and our students know the "answer" is sometimes just a click away. Volunteers have perspective to offer our children that helps them understand the relevance of their work. A volunteer sharing her travel experiences might help a child understand time zones. Another might explain how the garage he built could have fallen down if he had gotten the math wrong. They are providing students with real life examples of the content they are asked to learn. Volunteers help children understand the relevance of their work and their learning.

4.   **Hope.** *We need to provide an education for children that is hopeful.* It has been said that "80 percent of life is just showing up." When volunteers come into a classroom, they give our children hope by just showing up. A volunteer coming to the classroom says, *"I'm here because I'm interested in you."* Children look forward to interactions and time with the volunteer – and when they show up it gives them hope.

5.   **Meaning.** *We need to provide an education for children that is meaningful.* It is not only our responsibility to teach our children the importance of technology and the knowledge and experiences we have at our fingertips, it is also our responsibility to teach our children that the human experience will always be the most precious and most important of all. Volunteers provide meaningful human connections for our children.

Not only are these five "things" important for our children, but they are also the gifts the volunteer receives for his work. For those folks who are considering taking a step into the classroom, I would invite you to ask yourselves, *"What are the five things that matter to you?"* And, if anywhere among those five things there is a need to *be challenged and engaged, to feel relevant or hopeful, or to do something meaningful,* I would ask you to consider working with children in our schools. Not only can our students offer you all of those things, you will learn far more than you teach, you will receive more than you give, and you will smile far more than you ever have before.

STORY # 1 — WHY?

∞ ∞ ∞

Five decades ago I embarked on my plan to be a high school teacher and football coach. Just after I began a three-month student teaching experience in a Michigan junior high school, the regular teacher left for emergency surgery and I became the substitute teacher for the entire semester. I was a college senior and thought I knew more than I really did. I remember calling evening radio talk shows and expressing my opinions on world affairs; now I was trying to teach civics to classes of 7th graders. I was both frustrated and discouraged. My second teaching effort involved a summer program with three other teachers and 16 "gifted" kids in northern California. I concluded that the program's definition of "gifted" kids meant kids from wealthy families. Maybe I gave up too quickly. I changed direction in graduate school and prepared for entry into the Peace Corps and the Foreign Service.

Still, I've always been intrigued by those who choose to teach, especially elementary school teachers who are in charge of 20 kids for eight hours a day, five days a week. These teachers must have to field at least 200 questions a day. How is it done? How do teachers meet the education requirements, accommodate individual learning styles and multiple interests of students in the limited time available? How do they find a balance, engage each student, and create a positive learning environment? Fifty years later, I was about to find out.

When my eight-year-old grandson Aidan entered third grade at the Barrington Elementary School (BES), I attended an open house with his parents to meet his teacher, Ms. Canner. Aidan's new teacher shared plans for the year while giving a tour of her classroom. Her excitement for the new school year was contagious. And, as I would learn, she thoroughly enjoyed her daily task of challenging 17 eight-year-olds to learn.

Ms. Canner mentioned that a number of field trips were scheduled and adult chaperones were always in demand. "Do you think I should offer my services?" I asked Aidan's mother, Jessica, also an elementary school teacher. "Go for it!" she advised. "In fact, Ms. Canner might even welcome you as a classroom volunteer during the year." Being semi-retired and having the time, I thought, why not? At last here was my chance to discover, firsthand, how these teachers do their job. And little did I know that following my nine months with Ms. Canner's class, I would "graduate" with Aidan to Ms. Cowan's fourth grade class. I never imagined that my volunteer career would become a two-year stint.

Interestingly, my role as a volunteer was never really discussed or clearly defined with either teacher at the start. Instead, it evolved. Other volunteers assisted with specific subjects on a regular basis, or came in to help with special projects. My initial participation involved reading my book **Grammie Rules** (with Aidan) to the class, which led to a writing activity. Following that successful writing project, both Ms. Canner and Ms. Cowan invited me to be a part of the teaching team in a variety of subjects.

Throughout this book I mention rewards of the school volunteer experience in terms of benefits to the kids and help for the teachers. These rewards cover a broad spectrum. For example, I helped a fourth grader who was struggling with long division. Eventually she gained enough confidence to tell Ms. Cowan, "Now I can help teach other kids long division!" And there was the daily entry into the classroom and being greeted with a chorus of "Karl's here!" with an interruption of high fives and hugs. The brief celebration brought a smile to my face and the teachers were smiling, too. In 45 plus years of my working career, I don't recall ever hearing excited shouts of "Karl's here!" when I arrived for work.

Satisfying, rewarding, exciting, pleasing, fulfilling, worthwhile, edifying, and fruitful — all these descriptive words apply to my volunteer experience. Plus one more: fun. *It was just plain fun.* In writing **Karl's Here!** I hope my experiences will encourage others who might be interested in serving as a school volunteer. I had no idea how many rewards I would receive, personally. And maybe, just maybe, I made a small difference in these young students' lives and learning experience.

WHY DID I WRITE THIS BOOK?

My two-year volunteer experience was so much fun that I started to record my impressions. I simply wanted to remember the details of special events and activities, the reactions and comments of the teachers and kids, and my feelings about the rewards. I had almost finished scribbling notes for these stories when I asked myself: *Why and for whom am I writing?*

At first the answer seemed simple: I was writing for myself, personally. And to share with my two friends. That's enough of a reason, isn't it? But then I thought, well, perhaps it's also for my teachers — Ms. Canner and Ms. Cowan. Oh, and maybe Ms. Maxfield might enjoy reading it. Then there are my extended family members who, out of sympathy, will usually pick up a copy of whatever I write. Usually.

When I asked a retired elementary school teacher about a possible audience for my stories, she expressed the opinion that current teachers would find them of interest if they were considering volunteers for their classrooms. Maybe.

Then I said to myself, "Wait, Karl, if this opportunity has given you so much pleasure and satisfaction, obviously others could benefit from their own volunteer experience — particularly older adults, who have some extra of that most precious commodity called *time*."

There are many retired adults out there who value education and recognize that teachers need support and might welcome additional resources in the classroom. And, being very practical, volunteer manpower can help address increasing school costs and demands on school budgets. Retirees possess skills and knowledge that can make great contributions in subject areas like math, science, language arts, the arts, computer, and more. Some can share their hobbies, work career information, travels, and special interests to integrate into a curriculum unit in support of the teacher's effort.

Being a school volunteer was not on my initial list of priority retirement activities. This was in part, I think, because I had little understanding of how school volunteering works. And I certainly did not begin the experience with any preconceived notion about how I might fit into the program. Perhaps others are in that same situation, and if these stories about my own rewarding experiences reach and encourage other potential volunteers, then I'm glad I've written them to share. In my volunteer adventure, there were three winners – the kids, the teachers, and me, the volunteer.

STORY # 2 — THE SCHOOL SETTING
∞ ∞ ∞

Prior to my official classroom volunteer experience there, I had visited the BES many times. A retiree's resume includes the skill "available for drop off and pick up as needed." It was a skill that I had perfected. Ever since Aidan entered kindergarten, I was frequently enlisted to help Aidan's working parents. Visiting with others in the gym while waiting for dismissal was an enjoyable experience in itself. But then the bell would ring, my own grandkid would flash his big smile, run over to me with a hug, and launch into a detailed account of his day's adventures.

My actual classroom visits, however, had been limited to attending Aidan's "Show and Tell" nights. We would view and discuss the latest class project. I really paid little attention to the classroom setting itself, other than noting that there appeared to be an awful lot of "stuff" in it. When I began as a volunteer in the classroom, I soon learned how all that "stuff" actually had a purpose.

Along the way I discussed the idea of volunteering with four active school teachers, a retired school teacher, two mothers with kids in elementary schools, and one of my two friends, retired lawyer Stan. With the exception of Stan's, their responses were generally positive in terms of making a contribution by helping the teacher and students. They also mentioned possible "rewards," but I did not fully understand the rewards part until later. And I recall, they all suggested "You might have some fun."

Some expressed words of caution, and told stories of volunteers that didn't work out for various reasons: mismatch between volunteer and the teacher; expectations that were not fulfilled by either the teacher or volunteer (or both); lack of understanding of roles. The analogy to bad marriages was made frequently. I was told there are teachers who like the idea but often find that preparing for the volunteer's participation is more work than it is worth. I was cautioned there could be disappointment. And lawyer friend Stan was adamant. "Do not do it." But, despite his concerns about liability, which I kept in the back of my mind, I decided to go for it. Worst case scenario? I might fail, but at least I'd be able to cross it off my "things to try" list.

BES required that all school volunteers complete an application form and I was a bit apprehensive. My last application for acceptance – to MENSA – was rejected. But I passed the screening, and with Ms. Canner's blessing I became a BES volunteer.

Now, with two school years of volunteering behind me, I realize I owe my positive experience in large part to "my" two excellent teachers. Both Ms. Canner and Ms. Cowan were totally committed to maximizing the individual interests, strengths, and abilities of their volunteers to support their teaching efforts. They let the students know on day one – and always reinforced it – that the volunteer was part of the teaching team and was there to help.

Although we did not have lengthy discussions about their specific expectations of me, both teachers informally shared information with me about short- and long-term planned class activities. My roles just sort of evolved and when they introduced an activity to the class, the students were told that I would be available to help on certain aspects of the activity. As each year progressed, both teachers welcomed ideas for class projects that could relate to and be integrated into a planned learning unit, including literacy, math, and social studies.

VOLUNTEER AND TEACHER

The level of a volunteer's engagement in classroom activities is clearly defined by the individual teacher who often prepares the student in advance. My volunteer role, as explained to the students by Ms. Canner and Ms. Cowan, was often quite simple: "Karl's here today to help you." When the teacher's plan was to integrate a project idea into a learning unit, they told the students which aspects of this "Special and Fun Project" were my responsibility. It is important for the volunteer to recognize that assigned role, in order to play a supporting role to the teacher. *See Story #8 "Different Volunteer Roles."*

STORY # 3 — GRAMMIE RULES
∞ ∞ ∞

The summer before Aidan entered the second grade, I published **Grammie Rules: 49 Reasons to Spend Time with Your Grandkids.** The book includes stories about Aidan from birth through age seven. My volunteer role evolved after Ms. Canner invited me to read from the book to her third grade class. I had mentioned the book to her at an open house early in the school year. I suppose I appeared shameless and self-promoting, but Ms. Canner politely expressed interest in Aidan and extended the invitation to read . . . and that was the beginning of my volunteer experience.

The kids gathered on the classroom rug, while Aidan and I sat in front of the class. Ms. Canner explained, "Karl and Aidan will read today from a book that Karl has written about his relationship with Aidan."

The first response was incredulity. "You really wrote a book?" "A real book?" "A published book?" The reaction was a surprise to me until I realized that to many kids, the author is just a name on a book's cover. For most of them this was the first time they were actually talking with someone who had written a book. I explained that writing the book had been a lot of fun. I told them I had worked on the book for two years, and how pleased I was to share it with the class.

The second unexpected reaction came when I displayed the book, which features a picture of Aidan on the cover. "Wow, that's Aidan!" "Look, Aidan's on the cover!" "It is a book about Aidan." I should have anticipated the response. This was probably the first book about a person they knew, a classmate. The books they usually read, both fiction and nonfiction, are about people they don't know and probably will never meet. These were stories about a person, a real person they personally knew – one of them!

Aidan and I each selected three of our favorite stories and read them to an attentive audience of his peers. Following the reading, each student received a copy of **Grammie Rules** which Aidan and I autographed. It remained a popular read throughout the school year, especially during "Read to Self" and "Read with a Partner." And, this response came from several students: "My mom and dad loved **Grammie Rules.**"

The reading immediately prompted a sharing of stories from the students who were anxious to talk about things they did, their own experiences when they were "just little kids," and their relationships with their grandparents (and parents). Several expressed interest in being the subject of my next book, asking "Please, will you write a book about me?"

It became clear that it was not simply the writing that stimulated their interest. It was because it was a book about a subject (Aidan) to whom they could relate.

WHERE TO START

There is no "best" starting point for a volunteer to become involved with a class. That's really determined by the teacher, the volunteer's interests, and the planned classroom activities. For me, Grammie Rules worked well with both the third and fourth grade classes. The kids were excited to read the book and became interested in becoming authors. Both Ms. Canner and Ms. Cowan gave me several opportunities throughout the school year to help with class writing projects.

STORY # 4 — FIVE THINGS THAT MATTER
∞ ∞ ∞

Following the reading from **Grammie Rules,** the students expressed interest in being co-authors of a book and Ms. Canner proposed that we begin the project on my next visit. I rolled my eyes at Ms. Canner, who simply shrugged and gave me a "you suggested it" smile. I had my assignment, my first volunteer-directed project.

My next scheduled visit was only two days away, so I had to think of a suitable subject without delay. As chance would have it, totally unexpected help arrived. My nephew's wife Gwen sent me a piece that her third-grade daughter Alyda had written as an assignment. She and her classmates had each developed a list of "Five Things That Matter to Me." Alyda's list was both thoughtful and cute. The subject and title for Ms. Canner's group of authors-to-be had just been emailed to me!

In preparation for the project, I picked up 17 black and white 7 by 10 inch college composition books (perfect size with lined pages) and, of course, a No. 10 pencil for each student.

On my scheduled days, Ms. Canner usually listed "Karl's coming today" on the daily schedule that she posted each morning. Today she added "writing." It was too late to turn back. After briefly restating why we were beginning this activity, Ms. Canner turned to me and said, "It's all yours, Karl." Had I really waited 50 years for this?

The students gathered on the classroom rug and I introduced our project. I wanted them to be excited and encouraged, but also to be realistic about the often long process when writing. I used three rather global concepts, explaining that it would be a lot of hard work, assured them that it would also be fun, and promised that in the end the rewards of completing the project, of actually publishing a book, would make all the hard work worthwhile. We wrote "Hard Work" "Fun" "Rewards" on the board and frequently referred to those words. At the end of the project, each of the 17 students remembered those words verbatim and used them when asked about being authors!

Then we discussed the process: preparing a first draft, editing the draft, preparing a final draft, editing that draft, and then proofreading it before finally publishing. The new composition books and pencils were distributed (a big hit), and then came the question: "What are we going to write about?" Fortunately, I had learned from experience that sometimes you need to limit (or even prohibit) kids' choices and just tell them what to do. I elected that course of action with these 17 third graders, and announced the theme. "We (including Ms. Canner and me) are going to co-author a book entitled **FIVE THINGS THAT MATTER.**"

Hands shot up immediately. I was delighted they quickly bought into the idea. We spent four sessions working on their lists. Ms. Canner and I met with the students one-on-one or in small groups as they worked through their drafts and rewrites. Soon, even the two students who initially said "I don't like to write" and "I can't write" were among the active and excited participants.

Why not? They were expressing their own thoughts about a subject they knew better than anyone else. And there was the goal – to be a published book author!

Frankly, neither Ms. Canner nor I were concerned about what the students chose as their personal "things that matter." More important was their enthusiasm. They were engaged in writing and having fun creating their lists.

The subjects ranged from family to oxygen, from sports to school, from pets to Ms. Canner, and from the environment to food! When each one-page list was finally finished, Ms. Canner and I shared our own lists with the class.

Next we discussed the other components of a book. What about the cover? Did we need an introduction? Would a table of contents be a good idea? Ms. Canner provided a class picture for the book's cover. Then I collected the final lists and typed each student's page for the book. I delivered their collection to the local copy center and ordered 25 copies of the book. The kids had no idea we were printing multiple copies.

A few visits later I arrived at school bearing the finished product.

On my way past her office, I invited Ms. Maxfield to join Ms. Canner's class for a few minutes after recess. Now, Ms. Maxfield is one of those people who never seems to have a bad day and always finds every cup at least half full. She has a ready smile and quick wit, and is enthusiastic about students and their activities.

Of course, Ms. Maxfield already knew about the project, but the invitation to join the class was unplanned. She understood her attendance would be special for the class, so she quickly adjusted her schedule, saying she'd love to attend. I had gift-wrapped copies of the book for Ms. Canner and Ms. Maxfield and picked up a special gift for the principal. I arrived just before recess ended, put the gift-wrapped boxes on Ms. Canner's desk, and hid the large box with multiple copies of the book.

After returning from recess, Ms. Canner announced that Karl had something to share. I told them that their book was completed and we were waiting for a special guest to arrive to open the packages. I explained two packages were for our special guest and one for Ms. Canner to open – a copy of the book for their classroom. They were as excited as the day before summer vacation. I had just reminded the group that our guest would want to hear all about the process involved in the project they had completed, when, to their surprise, Ms. Maxfield arrived.

Ms. Maxfield and Ms. Canner opened their gifts – the final copy of the book, **FIVE THNGS THAT MATTER** and displayed to all the cover with their group picture.

Ms. Maxfield sat before the class as several students took turns explaining what goes into a book, how they had chosen the five things that mattered to them, and how they authored the book collectively. I was delighted they had remembered each step as well as our three concepts: hard work, fun, and rewards. Clearly Ms. Maxfield's excitement with their accomplishment equaled their own. With a proud "we did it" attitude, the kids settled on the classroom rug to watch Ms. Maxfield open her second gift. It contained a white tee shirt with the words **FIVE THINGS THAT MATTER** printed on it in black. The principal promised to wear it proudly.

The place was slightly out of control when I invited Ms. Maxfield to open the fourth and largest box. But nobody worried about control as the students realized the box contained more copies of the book – *one for each of them*. In a most jovial atmosphere, Ms. Maxfield presented each student (she knew every name) with his or her own personal copy of the book and congratulated each of them on becoming a published author.

A VOLUNTEER PROJECT

The book project is an example of how a volunteer can help complement a teacher's effort within a priority subject area. My availability provided Ms. Canner with additional adult support to complete a project that required expanded time with each student.

For me, the lucky volunteer, I had the satisfaction of designing and completing a successful project. I'm not sure even Ms. Canner was certain where it was headed when we started! What better words to hear from third graders? "I'm going to write more, it was fun!" and "I'm going to be an author." In subsequent weeks I encountered parents who told me how much their son or daughter enjoyed the experience. What else does a volunteer need?

Oh, and Ms. Canner? A year later she invited me back to work with her new third grade class. And yes, they upped the ante for the next group and co-authored "SIX THINGS THAT MATTER." And yes, Ms. Maxfield joined them for the launch.

STORY # 5 — TRANSITION
∞ ∞ ∞

Two weeks before the start of the new school year, I emailed Ms. Cowan to express my interest in volunteering with her new fourth grade class. I noted that my grandson Aidan would be in her class; I gave her Ms. Canner's name as my reference. When I didn't hear from Ms. Cowan until a few days before school started, I began to wonder if another short "teaching" career was over. I also wondered about my reference! My worrying ended when Ms. Cowan's email arrived. She would be delighted to have my volunteer involvement as soon as the class routine was set. Oh, and Ms. Canner had given me a strong endorsement.

The following week I attended the school's open house to meet the teachers and visited Ms. Cowan's classroom with Aidan and his family. After greeting Aidan and his parents, Ms. Cowan turned to me, smiled politely, and said, "So *you* must be Karl. How about coming in next week?" It was my shortest, most successful job interview ever.

I was a bit apprehensive about my first session with the new class. Would this year be as exciting and rewarding as the previous one? Ms. Canner and I had developed a relationship that worked well. I understood my role and her expectations. Could something similar be developed with Ms. Cowan and her class? And there were 18 new kids to get to know. Aidan and his friend Trevor were the only students who moved with me from Ms. Canner's third grade. Eighteen new kids. How would they respond to me? I was accustomed to that daily greeting, "Karl's here!" and the high fives and hugs, and Ms. Canner's welcoming smile when I arrived. I was nervous. What was ahead?

Thanks to Ms. Cowan, I can report that my transition from the third to the fourth grade could not have gone better. Ms. Cowan's introduction was perfect. "This is Aidan's grandfather and Aidan is going to share Karl with us as a volunteer during the year. Karl will help during literacy and writing units and other subjects and activities." *Perfect.* "Karl has written several books, including a book about Aidan, which maybe he will share with us." *Perfect.*

MUTUAL EXPECTATIONS

My impression is that a teacher and a volunteer can develop a plan for collaboration in virtually every classroom setting. The interests of the volunteer and the needs of the teacher can be accommodated to benefit the students. There are so many activities and tasks to be completed that success is highly likely.

STORY # 6 — YOU DID WHAT?

∞ ∞ ∞

Ms. Cowan unknowingly had already laid the ground work for my first fourth grade assignment. The students had begun to write on the topic "How I Spent My Summer Vacation." It would prove to be the perfect assignment for the class to become co-authors of a book.

During my next classroom visit, Aidan and I read from **Grammie Rules.** Then the kids shared stories about their own childhood experiences. The reaction to our reading was similar to the response from Ms. Canner's third graders. This was the first time for most that they knew a book's subject (Aidan) personally and had a chance to meet the author (Karl). We did the book distribution and signing and yes, the group agreed it would be fun to write a book.

We discussed the idea of expanding the "summer vacation" assignment into a book. The individual stories could be compiled so the kids could be co-authors. I outlined the writing and publishing process, and introduced the theme "Hard Work, Fun, and Rewards."

To help the class understand the steps involved in this book-writing project, I prepared a grid on a 2 by 3 foot poster board. Student names were listed down the left column, and across the top I listed the eight steps they must complete to become published authors. The poster was a big hit as the students could track their own writing progress by adding a star in the appropriate box after each step was completed and approved by either Ms. Cowan or Karl.

Step one was to have an "idea." They all received the first star immediately. Only seven more steps to go:

- Write a first draft
- Review and edit
- Prepare a second draft
- Review and edit
- Complete a final draft
- Proofread
- Publish

The students found it exciting to see stars appear on the board

14

behind their names as they completed each step – another step closer to their goal of being published authors.

Over a three-week period, time was allotted to work on their story drafts, meeting one-on-one periodically with Ms. Cowan or me to work through their drafts. We emphasized grammar and spelling, subjects Ms. Cowan would work on throughout the school year. We encouraged these writers to add interesting details to their story, and to explain why they enjoyed a particular activity. We asked them to include what they had learned, and whether they would choose to do this again next summer.

The stories were fun to read. They traveled by airplane, car, boat, and bus and visited more than 20 states, from Connecticut to Alaska and from Vermont to Florida. They spent time with their relatives and friends. They stayed in hotels, motels, and lake cabins. They spent time at lakes and forests. They ate at different types of restaurants. They visited large and small museums. They completed personal projects with individual accomplishments. They attended sporting events and actively participated in many different sports. They attended concerts. They had many first time experiences and visited places they had only previously seen in pictures.

After they completed their final drafts in their coveted new black 7 by 10 inch college composition books, I typed each story, double spaced for their final proofreading and any last minute changes. We also had them proofread each other's stories in pairs. The proofreading proved to be a popular step in the process. They challenged each other to have their stories without spelling errors and the correct punctuation. Interestingly, the students remembered the proofreading exercise in future writing projects.

We collaborated on the other components of the book – the cover (with a class picture), introduction, and table of contents. Earlier I had mentioned that sometimes a book in progress has a "working title." Did they want to use "How I Spent My Summer Vacation," or consider alternatives? That option set off a lively debate as the students brainstormed and listed several alternatives on the board, eliminating the suggestions through group voting. They wanted something catchy and settled on the title **YOU DID WHAT?! How 20 Students Spent a Fun Summer Vacation in 2013** by Ms. Cowan's

2013–14 Fourth Grade Class.

I typed the final copy and ordered 25 printed copies. I told the kids a couple of copies would be made for their classroom, and a copy for the school library. But I did not reveal that they would each receive a personal copy.

I invited Ms. Maxfield to join the class for the publication party. While the kids were at recess, I delivered the carton of books to the classroom along with a large sheet cake decorated with the words: **YOU DID WHAT?!** Ms. Cowan's Fourth Grade 2013-14. When they returned from recess, the kids were met with Ms. Maxfield's surprise entrance. "I understand that I am entering a room of published authors!" She received a resounding cheer at that announcement. The students couldn't wait to display the chart and eagerly explained in detail the process that led to their accomplishment. Ms. Maxfield inquired about each step and the work involved. Was it a test? Hmmm. They passed with flying colors, and reminded Ms. Maxfield of the "hard work, fun, and rewards" of being an author.

Ms. Maxfield scanned through the pages, commented on several of the stories, and assured the students **YOU DID WHAT?!** would be her priority reading for that evening. I presented the box of books to her and asked if she would be willing to do the honors. She made their day as she handed each student a copy of the book and offered her congratulations to each on being a published author. The autograph party – with cake – followed.

VOLUNTEER REWARDS

While discussing the steps in writing the book, Ms. Maxfield asked the kids, "What part was the most fun?" Many replied enthusiastically, "Working with Karl." Ms. Cowan and I exchanged knowing smiles.

Ms. Maxfield and I stood in the back of the room while the kids ate cake and autographed their page for their classmates. She turned to me and said, "Thank you, Karl, for doing this."

STORY # 7 — COMMON CORE STANDARDS
∞ ∞ ∞

"Core requirements," "standard achievement tests," "measured progress," and "common core." Wow, these terms certainly were not a part of my working career vocabulary. But the terms are part of everyday teacher conversations, used frequently when explaining assignments to students. They appear on student work sheets and tests. They are an integral part of the classroom environment and learning process.

I include these comments about Common Core because a school volunteer will quickly recognize the impact that the core requirements have on how time is allocated during the school day. Clearly, among teachers there are mixed reactions to the myriad of standards and requirements.

The school volunteer experience triggered a new reading topic for me. Like many non-educators, I had learned bits and pieces about President Bush's No Child Left Behind Act of 2001 and President Obama's Race to the Top in 2009. Since 2010, considerable media attention has been given to the Common Core State Standards initiatives in math and reading. As a classroom volunteer, I observed firsthand how these mandates impact classroom procedures and schedules. I was curious, so I selected at least a dozen articles to read about this Common Core activity. That reading, plus my own classroom observations, gave me a better understanding of the "whys" and "hows" of Common Core. And it helped me better understand when and how I could be helpful to the teacher in her efforts to meet the requirements.

I tried to recall my elementary school days during the years when Harry Truman was President. I remember the names of my elementary school teachers, but I admit that a completely accurate recollection of the actual learning experience is difficult. That said, I know that my educational experience was quite different than what I observe today. There was structure, but with more leeway, more flexibility for the teacher. I don't remember taking so many tests. I remember that our core curriculum included reading, writing, arithmetic, science, and social studies. And we learned cursive writing by copying a single short sentence on the blackboard until it was judged to be acceptable. We memorized multiplication and division tables at school and practiced at home. Yes, a very different time.

The education delivery system has changed dramatically in our rapidly changing world. The kids use laptop computers; we used the slide rule. We went to the library's card catalog and found a book in the library stacks; they "Google." Recognizing and being open to the new learning environment will help the volunteer to understand better where he/she can help both the teacher and the students.

THE COMMON CORE VOLUNTEER

Meeting the fourth grade math requirements meant a significant amount of individualized instruction time was needed for each student to master the skills to score well on the standardized test. The process offered numerous opportunities for me to help Ms. Cowan and Ms. Tessier, a paraprofessional who assisted during math allotment periods. When the students were assigned to specific "centers" to work on math, I might be assigned to work with three or four students, or respond to a student's request for extra help while working solo at his/her desk. In this volunteer role, I know I made an important contribution to the math program.

STORY # 8 — DIFFERENT VOLUNTEER ROLES
∞ ∞ ∞

During my volunteering, I enjoyed sharing my "school stories" with other adults. My stories were about funny things that happened in the classroom, or priceless comments and observations that only eight- to ten-year-olds make. There really was something different each day.

I would suggest to other retirees that they might consider school volunteering themselves, at some point. The most frequent responses? "I've never taught." "I haven't been in a school in 40 plus years." "Me do new math?" Once I moved beyond the easy answers to those concerns and questions, we discussed the variety of roles that a school volunteer could choose.

I profess no expertise on the subject. However, I want to share a few observations based on my two-year experience as a classroom volunteer. They might help a reader who is wondering, "Could there really be a role for me?" Here are three scenarios that describe ways a volunteer can contribute to the kids' classroom experience and be a valuable resource to the teacher.

First, there is general assistance. A volunteer can relieve the teacher of dozens of tasks: photocopying, organizing and distributing materials, running errands, responding to individual questions ("Can I go to the bathroom?"). This type of help allows a teacher to focus on the primary mission of educating the kids. And there is helping the teacher stay on schedule. This will not surprise anyone who has experienced the challenge (and frustration) of getting their own children ready for school in the morning! Now multiply that task by 18 to 20 kids when preparing to make the switch from, say, a reading group to a math session. Questions are asked and prodding is needed. "Where is your book?" "Your pencil?" "Put away what is on your desk!" "Yes, you can go to the bathroom, but hurry!" Yes, a volunteer can assist with this transition.

Second, be a volunteer and assist on a designated day for a specific period of time to assist with a specific teaching unit. The volunteer is filling a role much like a teacher's aide. For example, the volunteer visits every Tuesday and Thursday to help when students are working on assignments in their math workbook. Or, it can be during a period of time when a couple of things are regularly scheduled (reading, working on a special project, etc.) and the teacher can count on the volunteer's help with an assigned role.

This role is fun as it can involve varied tasks and subjects. For example, on a given afternoon I would read *Scholastic News* aloud at a table with a group of students (each reading a paragraph) and then lead the discussion of the material we read. I was always able to introduce some personal experience relating to the subject, which contributed to the learning process. On a few occasions we even held a contest to determine if my group could remember more than Ms. Canner's group! Following the reading, I then switched gears and helped a small group of students complete their assigned math workbook pages.

As a third option, the volunteer can assume a lead role on a longer term project extending over a 3- to 4-week period. I was offered this opportunity with student writing units in both the third and fourth grade classes. The opportunities for adult volunteers are unlimited in this scenario. Elementary school kids are exposed to dozens of subjects and topics during the school year. Sure, there are the traditional reading, writing, and arithmetic (OK, *math*). But the school curriculum encompasses an array of subjects from history to current events. The special interests, career experience, and skills of the volunteer can be utilized to complement a teaching unit. Are there history buffs out there? Retirees with government experience? A passion for endangered species, weather, coin collecting, arts and crafts, plants and gardening, space travel, automobiles, poetry, media? All can be integrated into the classroom experience.

I offer a personal example. After my postage stamp collection had gathered dust for three decades, I found an opportunity to use those old stamps in the classroom in four projects. Both Ms. Canner and Ms. Cowan saw my stamp-related activities as a "fun" learning experience for their students. The most elaborate project involved research and writing with the fourth graders. *See Story #13 "Postage Stamps."* The stamp projects planned for Christmas and Valentine's Day were for many students their first exposure to the history and use of postage stamps. Yes, there was communication before the internet!

EVERY VOLUNTEER ACTIVITY COUNTS

I found that even the small roles or short-term projects make major contributions to the classroom. They support the teacher's efforts and compliment the required educational requirements. And for the volunteer? Sharing a special avocation or personal interest, perhaps a lifelong hobby or career experience, can be a rewarding adventure. It is especially exciting when a new interest is kindled for a student.

STORY # 9 — MATH MASTER

∞ ∞ ∞

Both Ms. Canner and Ms. Cowan allowed me to work independently with their classes on what Ms. Canner labeled "Special and Fun Projects." One of the kids' favorites was a game I called "Math Master" (no, I have not patented the game). We first played it during my volunteer days with Ms. Canner's third grade and again by popular demand, the next year in Ms. Cowan's fourth grade.

Math Master complemented the teaching of basic math to the third and fourth graders. When I was a kid it was a game my mother played with me and my two brothers almost every day. Our version was very competitive because the loser had to do extra household chores!

With so much emphasis on mastery of math skills, I was looking for a "Special and Fun Project" that would excite the students, would be something they *wanted* to do. I wanted a game with no losers, a game where each could be successful regardless of math skill level, and when completed at least some of the students might say, "That math activity was cool!" Math Master achieved all of that – and more.

Our game board was a 2 by 3 foot poster with the students' names in a column on the left side and the five playing "rounds" across the top: Round 1, Round 2, Round 3, Semifinals, and Finals. The students gathered on the classroom rug. When his or her name was called, that student would stand and I would give the player an oral math problem (for example, 3 plus 3 plus 1 take away 5 times 5 plus 2 minus 3). The student would calculate the answer in his/her head. Their classmates would also work the problem and wait anxiously to hear the correct answer. With the correct answer, a designated scorekeeper put a check on the game board for that round after the student's name. For each round, the problem became more complex and I increased the speed with which I asked the question.

I added two rules for the class version of Math Master to keep the game challenging. I think that strategy increased Math Master's popularity and helped create excitement. The first rule was that each student had to be successful in each round in order for the entire class to win the championship. The class played against itself, and the overall goal was for the entire class to be "Team Champion." There would be a prize for each member of the team if, and only if, each student answered all five of his or her problems correctly during the course of the game. Because individual success was needed for team success, as we progressed through each round, the cheers became louder, with a resounding "YES!" for the correct answers, with high fives all around. "The pressure is on," I'd announce frequently. "The correct answer is needed or no winner!" My comments produced words of encouragement from the class members as the next student prepared to give an answer. "Come on, you can do it! You can do it!"

The second rule was that in each round the final participant for the team was the teacher. In each class the excited students expressed their encouragement. "You just have to get it right for us to be winners," they reminded the teacher. Then they waited breathlessly for her to give the correct answer. And two teachers, whose popularity ratings from their students were already high, found their ratings skyrocket.

We introduced Math Master only after I'd been a volunteer for a couple of months in each class. During that time I obtained a fairly good sense of each student's math skill level and was able to design the difficulty of each student's problem accordingly. Obviously, I wanted them to calculate the correct answer. But just as importantly, it was also an opportunity for students to build confidence doing math with their peers. In addition, following its establishment as a Special and Fun Project, Math Master became one of the most popular games of choice when students had free activity time.

Oh, the game results? The students in each class were winners, "Team Champions." In both the third and fourth grade game versions, the final championship round was particularly filled with tension. There was a joyous celebration when Ms. Canner and Ms. Cowan produced their team's clinching correct answer. Of course, there were rewards, always popular with students. The third graders were delighted with their reward – a new activity book and box of crayons for each. The fourth graders celebrated with the $5 gift card to Dunkin Donuts that they each received.

VOLUNTEER DIRECTED PROJECT

Math Master is an example of a "Special and Fun Project — an activity where a volunteer can really have fun too, engaging and interacting with the students. For the students, the activity offers a change from regular school work and is "directed" by someone other than the regular teacher. The kids react a little differently to the volunteer who is playing a teaching role. The volunteer is perceived as a guest, a helper, a friend, and a support arm to the teacher. I can't explain the kids' positive responses. But judging from the results of Math Master, there was full attention and 100 percent effort by each student. They wanted to give the right answer to satisfy themselves, to support their classmates, and, I think, to show Karl that "I can do it." What other reward could a volunteer ask for?

STORY # 10 — THE ONE-ON-ONE VOLUNTEER
∞ ∞ ∞

Of the various rewarding roles a school volunteer can play, working one-on-one with a student deserves special mention. The one-on-one arrangement is extremely beneficial to the student and provides helpful support to the teacher.

The demand for this individual assistance is significant. The reality is that most students will need additional help in at least one subject area during the school year. I am not referring to the work of certified special education staff. Rather, I refer to the basic day-to-day work (reading, writing, and math) in which all students are engaged. Some kids simply grasp new concepts more quickly than others. Some struggle with a specific subject. With extra one-on-one attention, the student who needs help has an increased chance of moving ahead on the learning curve.

An example: The teacher introduces a new math "concept," finding the area and perimeter of shapes (Okay, I admit I needed a fast refresher from Ms. Cowan before I could help). Then, examples are discussed and work sheets are distributed to the students to work independently. Ms. Cowan would say, "Raise your hand if you need help from either of us." You don't have to be a math major to realize that the teaching capacity doubles when a volunteer is also available to provide help for the students. When most of the class was ready to continue, Ms. Cowan could move the class forward while I continued to work with those who needed more practice.

Another example: Research projects present a perfect opportunity for a volunteer to provide one-on-one assistance for a student. Ms. Canner's third graders each selected a state to research for a report. They each were provided a large state map and general guidelines for the report. They located information in library books and, of course, through computer searching. My role was to help them narrow the scope of the inquiry and to obtain relevant information about the state. Points of interest, famous people, population trends, and natural resources were some of their topics. My availability meant that each could have more individual guidance from an adult.

Final example: Writing units provide opportunities for one-on-one.

In the fourth grade the students did one writing project using "persuasive" words. The students had lists of words to use for each assignment. When I met one-on-one with a student we would discuss the words, selecting those that might help persuade the reader. The words included on the list were: you, free, because, instantly, new, sensational, guaranteed, superior, and tremendous. They used them all!

Quick story. The persuasive writing assignment required each student to write a letter to his/her parents requesting a new, exotic, house pet. The pet selections ranged from snakes to elephants and *every* animal in between. It was a perfect opportunity to discuss how you persuade someone. Their suggestions ranged from why the pet would benefit the household to flattery: "You're such wonderful parents." I agreed to write my own persuasive letter. It was to Ms. Cowan and I shared it with the class the next day. I offered 10 reasons why "the best fourth grade teacher in the world" should allow us to have a class pet. My tenth reason? "You just have to say yes because the pet is already in the classroom!" The kids were stunned. "You mean you have our pet here? Here in the room?" Neither Ms. Cowan nor the kids noticed that I had brought in a box that contained a small fish bowl and a fish. The kids opened the box gently, then immediately shouted, "No way can Ms. Cowan say no!" The vote was unanimous to keep the fish (20 students and Karl). Ms. Cowan had no choice but to agree. The students were very creative in writing their own persuasive letters. Many parents wrote back to compliment their child's persuasive letter, explaining regretfully that they had to refuse the request. Persuading parents to accept a rhino or giraffe was a difficult assignment, but a good writing experience.

VOLUNTEER SKILLS NEEDED: AVAILABILITY AND PATIENCE

I did not bring any special skills to the classroom to provide one-on-one assistance. I simply became a "student" when the teacher explained the project and then took her lead. She would give me a crash course when needed; for example, when the method for teaching a particular math skill was not familiar to me. I also learned that patience is certainly a virtue when working one-on-one. You are so eager for "your" student to "get it." And yes, when the "aha!" moment does finally arrive for the student, it is gratifying for you, too.

STORY # 11 — LAS VEGAS

∞ ∞ ∞

No, I did not run a training session on gambling or lead a discussion about Las Vegas shows. But Las Vegas was one of our Special and Fun Projects, and it was an unusual learning experience.

Our study of Las Vegas and Nevada was a sequel to a research project for which each student had completed a report on a specific state. I especially enjoyed the project as I could help by sharing information about my travels throughout the U.S. and the five states in which I had resided – Michigan, Washington, Arizona, Oregon, and New Hampshire. Each of those states had been selected by a student.

We spent additional time studying Nevada because I was leaving for a week's vacation in Las Vegas. I shared my trip itinerary and brought in a half dozen oversized picture books about Las Vegas and Nevada. The books were a popular addition to the classroom library for the remainder of the school year.

We located on maps areas such as Sloan Canyon, Hoover Dam, and Lake Mead, places of interest in and around the city of Las Vegas, and we discussed other Nevada attractions. We learned about the formation of the Grand Canyon, made comparisons of its size to other places; the weather at the top and bottom of the Canyon on a given day; the mule trips for visitors to the bottom of the Canyon; and the amazing view from a recently completed lookout with a glass bottom that extends out over the Canyon. They were fascinated by the stories about the building of Hoover Dam, and my trip to the base of the dam on an elevator that operates inside the dam. I spent time talking about Red Rock Canyon National Conservation Area, my favorite non-casino site in Nevada, located just northeast of Las Vegas. I take a day trip to Red Rock Canyon on every trip to the city. We discussed the frequently spotted wild horses and small reptiles in the area, the unique rock formations, and how the rocks received their red color. I described how plant life survives, the flash floods and wildfires that occur, and the eerie quietness you experience when walking deep into the remote area.

And yes, we talked about Elvis, the large and colorful casinos, and a brief introduction to the dos and don'ts of gambling!

Each day during my travels I mailed several postcards to the class, depicting the places we had discussed. All visitors to Las Vegas return with souvenirs, and 17 third graders were expecting one from me! I brought back two small cardboard slot machines, which contained a gold-wrapped chocolate dollar for each student. Very popular. Another big hit was a $1 casino playing chip, which each received and decided to keep as a good luck charm. A very small piece of red rock from the Canyon was handled like grandma's priceless China glassware. But the most popular gift? A 30-minute video about Red Rock Canyon National Conservation Area that we watched together.

VIVA LAS VEGAS

The Las Vegas focus could have been a rather narrow learning experience, but we broadened it with discussions about how much fun it is to learn about places and people when traveling. I shared information about the desert, climate, and the different lifestyle in Las Vegas. Having made numerous trips to Las Vegas, it was easy for me to answer question from curious kids. Most senior citizens have resided in several different places and can bring knowledge and real experiences about those places to the classroom. And it is fun to relive those memories and share personal experiences.

STORY # 12 — FIELD TRIPS
∞ ∞ ∞

Field trips are an important part of the learning process for elementary school children. No story, reading assignment, or group discussion can match the field trip experience. Words can describe a place, but walking, seeing, and touching the surroundings, will make it real. The kids look forward to these adventures with excitement and great anticipation. Teachers consider the educational value when planning a field trip, but they also have to make sure all students get there *and* get back!

Field trips are an excellent opportunity for volunteer participation because chaperones are always needed. The volunteers provide additional sets of eyes and ears for the teacher when assigned responsibility for the well-being of a small group of students. And yes, riding the school bus brings back memories!

I accompanied Ms. Canner's third graders on two field trips. The first was to the Boston Museum of Science. We had four volunteers and each was responsible for four students. The volunteers were given a list of their responsibilities and schedule details. The challenge was to guide the four kids through a dozen "must see" displays at the Museum *and* stay on schedule. The kids' inquisitive nature took control, of course, which was great, and I made at least 10 head counts to be sure my four were with me at all times. We survived. Everyone had fun, including this volunteer.

The second field trip adventure involved a visit to the Waste Management (WM) regional disposal facilities and a nature walk. The class was studying environmental issues and how individuals can contribute through recycling. WM had developed marvelous public walking trails along a river near their facility. During the walk students discussed the need to protect the environment, including the river, and habitats of birds and fish. The WM tour was informative for all. The students and volunteers were equally fascinated to observe the facility with its huge packing machines and deep holes for burying treated waste. Oh, and only one student slipped into the river, but she climbed out with no worse than soaked walking shoes. A fun (and educational) day for everyone.

SMILE

Amy and I were responsible for six kids on the nature walk portion of the trip. I'd met Amy (and her great sense of humor) previously. Aidan and her son Brendan were good friends. When I was a little late boarding the school bus, the students greeted me with "Karl's here!" Amy just rolled her eyes and gave me a look that said, "What's this about?" I whispered, "It's great. Makes me feel like a rock star." Amy didn't miss a beat: "Yeah, Mick Jagger."

STORY # 13 — POSTAGE STAMPS
∞ ∞ ∞

For almost 40 years, I was an avid stamp collector, accumulating over one million U.S. postage stamps. I had purchased dozens of boxes of used stamps, bought two significant private collections, and even published an article about stamp collecting.

My philately hobby lay dormant for almost 25 years, until my semi-retirement. At last I had time to sort the collection. I retained stamps with value and discarded the rest – except for a half dozen shoe boxes crammed with used stamps. I kept them because my grandkids, like my daughters before them, loved playing with my old postage stamps. They decorated drawings and greeting cards, and sorted stamps by subjects. I never imagined that those postage stamps would be utilized for a volunteer-led class project with third and fourth graders!

I suspected that Ms. Canner's third graders would have the same enthusiasm as my grandkids did for the stamps. I brought in a single shoe box of 10,000 stamps for Show and Tell. It proved to be a big hit. We had a discussion about U.S. postage stamps in preparation for one of Ms. Canner's "Special and Fun Projects." During the holiday season, each student drew an evergreen tree and decorated it with stamps of their choice, including commemorative Christmas stamps. Interestingly, virtually every student asked if they could take stamps home. Some wanted to start a stamp collection. Some simply wanted to show their parents. One student was interested in collecting stamps featuring U.S. Presidents. I had mentioned that some older stamps have value to collectors and many were prepared to search for that elusive upside down airplane. "I'm going to find one that will help pay my way through college," said one eight year-old with determination.

A year later we did an expanded project with postage stamps in Ms. Cowan's fourth grade. I drew a large evergreen tree on a poster board, assigned a branch to each student, and they selected their favorite stamps from the collection to paste on their branch. When her students expressed interest in the postage stamps, Ms. Cowan invited me to lead a research and writing project about U.S. postage stamps.

Most of the students were not very familiar with postage stamps. In fact, few had used postage stamps except for holiday cards, birthday cards, and thank you notes. I explained that a great deal can be learned about the U.S. and its history by studying the people and places featured on the stamps. We discussed the history of the U.S. Postal Service and how postage stamps are created. Our discussion of mail delivery allowed me to share one of my favorite topics, the Pony Express. A popular discussion involved the original cost and current value of old stamps. I brought in a used stamp with a catalog price of $500, a big hit! They had fun guessing the best-selling stamps of all time (Elvis, the LOVE stamp). They learned how subjects are selected for stamps, the criteria used, and the design selected. And they had a great time suggesting celebrities who should be honored with their own commemorative postage stamps. Their suggestions ranged from New England Patriots quarterback Tom Brady to the popular singer Taylor Swift! Fun stuff.

To begin the research and writing phase of the project, each student selected a favorite stamp from the collection. I prepared a research outline that required answers to several questions: (1) When was the stamp issued? (2) What are its dimensions? (3) What was the stamp's original value? (4) What is its value today? (5) Why did you select the stamp? Based on their research, they each wrote a brief narrative about the stamp, including why it was an important enough subject to warrant its own postage stamp. I worked individually with each student to review the information and together we edited the narrative. They were totally engaged.

There were many interesting aspects to this project, including the reasons students gave for selecting a particular stamp. One student selected Martin Luther King, Jr., saying "He helped with civil rights." Another picked Eleanor Roosevelt because they shared the same birth date. James Naismith was selected because basketball was one student's favorite sport. Places they had visited and animals were popular selections.

I collected their work, typed each one-page report in the format of the research outline, and pasted the selected stamp on the report page. I prepared a cover for the whole project with the title **Postage Stamp Research and Writing Project** by Ms. Cowan's Fourth Grade Class. The Table of Contents included each student's name and the research subject of his or her selected stamp. Unknown to the students and Ms. Cowan, I ordered 25 copies of each page printed, then collated and bound into individual booklets.

I brought the booklets to the classroom and totally surprised 20 fourth graders. They were proud and excited. Why not? They were holding the results of their own research efforts. Ms. Cowan gave the group extended time to autograph their pages, and to read to each other from their new booklets.

During other projects with these students, I had emphasized that proofreading was one of the most important steps in writing. However, apparently I was a bit careless in typing the postage stamp reports. During a half hour of reading their booklets to each other, at least half the class took great delight in pointing out three misspelled words, three typos, and two punctuation errors. Plus I had glued a stamp upside down on one page. Lesson learned!

HIGH FIVE

In addition to watching the kids read and discuss their work, my first reward came from Ms. Cowan. She looked at me after the booklet distribution, shook her head, and said with a high five, "I can't believe you prepared that book." Ah, the satisfaction of being a volunteer . . . and the advantage of having time.

STORY # 14 — LBJ

∞ ∞ ∞

Ms. Cowan's fourth grade class was working on a research/writing project based on old U.S. postage stamps. Chris told me that he'd chosen to do his report on the Lyndon B. Johnson eight-cent commemorative stamp issued in 1974. Chris said he made the selection "Because President Johnson is my dad's favorite President."

During the 10-minute class snack time, a period when Ms. Cowan often invited me to share a story or idea with the class, I told the class about Chris's postage stamp choice and asked for a show of hands. "Who can identify Lyndon Johnson?" Three of the 20 students were able to identify LBJ as a former President. "What?" I said to myself. I was shocked. But then I remembered the two generation gaps. LBJ served 40 years before these nine-year-olds were even born!

And other teaching moment for me had arrived. I've always had a special interest in the U.S. Presidency, and I was excited. Here was my opening to help the kids learn about LBJ, and a chance to contribute a personal story.

I elected to tell the kids about the time I shook hands with President Johnson. It was in 1964 during his campaign visit to Arizona. I was working as an administrative intern with the Phoenix city government. President Johnson was running against a fellow named Barry Goldwater. As circumstances would have it, I also had a chance to step inside Air Force One at the Phoenix Airport while the President was in the city making a campaign speech. I described LBJ as a big man – he was 6'5" tall, with very large hands, and I mimicked his Texas drawl for them. Just his presence was overwhelming. After all, I was only 24 years old and this was *the* President of the United States. Suddenly, I was aware of dead silence in the room as 20 fourth graders sat spellbound at their desks, snacks forgotten, listening intently to my LBJ story.

I told the kids they would likely meet a U.S. President one day and asked how they thought they'd feel. Two reported accompanying their parents to see President Obama during his visit to New Hampshire. Others reported seeing President Bush's house in Maine, and seeing the White House on a trip to D.C. They were deeply engaged in a discussion of the Presidency. My LBJ story had piqued their interest and produced a barrage of questions about Air Force One, the Secret Service, other Presidents I might have met, whether I had met any First Ladies, etc. I promised them more another day if there was time – and with Ms. Cowan's approval. Ms. Cowan's popularity remained high as she assured them it would be possible.

Several weeks later when the class was sharing their completed postage stamp reports, I asked again for a show of hands: "Who was Lyndon Johnson?" Yes, there was 100 percent recognition. Mission accomplished!

THE VOLUNTEER'S PERSONAL EXPERIENCE

Kids learn best from personal stories about history. At least I recall more about the Great Depression and WW II from my mother's stories than from history books. Her descriptions of standing in line with ration coupons for flour and dry milk were more vivid and real to me than written words or pictures.

Seniors have lived through periods of history that can come alive when they share their own personal experiences. This added dimension of real life stories can make an abstract topic more relatable. The kids were intrigued to hear about my phone call with Jimmy Carter, a luncheon with Eleanor Roosevelt, and an awards ceremony with Gerald Ford. They were not impressed by my contact with Spiro Agnew.

STORY # 15 — STORIES FOR THE CLASS
∞ ∞ ∞

"Writing is fun when you write about something you know or experience or just think about."

I wish that quote was from a famous author. Unfortunately, it's mine, one that I repeated frequently to the third and fourth grade students.

I was impressed with the students' great enthusiasm for reading. I mean every student! They received encouragement and were given opportunities to read every day during periods of "Read to Self" and "Read Aloud with a Classmate." The kids read everywhere – at their desks, on the floor, sitting in the corner. And those backpacks they carry to school every day? On the day the kids had their library "special," the backpacks were extra heavy going home.

I wanted to connect their love for reading with their writing potential. We discussed how, with continued efforts, eventually they could write stories and books that others would want to read. Because I know writing is a challenge for most of us, I was ready to counter their complaints: "It's hard to write," and "I don't know how to say it." I explained that it helps when you write about something you've seen, ideas that you think about, or a personal experience. "You can write it better than anyone else," I told them. "After all, it's your story."

I asked myself: "How can I show these kids what I'm talking about, and encourage them to express it in writing?" I decided to use myself as an example. I explained to the class that I always keep a small notebook handy, and frequently write notes to myself. Those notes often led to an article that I'd write later. I encouraged them to do the same and brought in a small spiral-bound notebook for each.

Periodically I would write a 300- to 400-word story and read it to the class. The stories were written in the first person with the title "WHAT AM I?" or "WHO ARE WE?" The kids could relate to the topics. I chose to illustrate types of creative humor they could appreciate.

I handed a copy of the story to each student and then read it aloud to the class. At the conclusion they would guess what or who was the subject of the story. There were many opportunities during this writing project to remind them that they could have a lot of fun writing similar stories.

Oh, the topics of the stories I wrote? Here is one example: "I was resting quietly in the front closet when my owner came and took me out. It was time to go to work." "I" was a suitcase who got thrown around, left behind in the airport, was eventually reunited with his owner, and did its job. After the students collectively guessed "I" was a suitcase, one student said he could write about when the airlines lost the family luggage.

This is another: "I am unique. I move through the atmosphere, bumping into my friends with many cries of 'ouch.' I get caught in updrafts and downdrafts, and eventually settle on the ground to disappear." "I" is a snowflake. A student said she was going to write a similar story about a raindrop.

The kids' favorite story was about a year in the life of a plant bulb. The bulb was planted and fed regularly. She eventually emerged and during the summer had many visitors, including school children, who would talk about her and even touch her. But the children returned to school, the days became shorter, and she knew her days were numbered. In fact, the bulb knew her final day had arrived when she overhead the gardener say that on Saturday he planned to cut her head off. But she knew she'd be back in the spring. One student said, "I'm going to write a story about my life as a tree."

Yes, I was reminded over and over that there are only 60 minutes in an hour. We never had time to pursue this story initiative, but the students were excited and motivated by the "WHAT AM I?" idea. Two students reported using their notebooks to keep a diary of a family trip, another wrote about a sporting event in which she participated, and another wrote a fictional story about a four-wheeler. Perhaps this will be a good writing project for another year.

VOLUNTEER INITIATIVES

Teachers have the constraints of work that *must* be completed during the school year. Volunteers do not have constraints. They have opportunities to bring something a little different to the classroom and need only the teacher's approval to try it. Both Ms. Canner and Ms. Cowan supported the "let's try it" approach with efforts like "Stories for the Class."

STORY # 16 — A BOOK OF STORIES TO COME
∞ ∞ ∞

Hindsight is 20-20. I wish I'd made daily notes of student comments and conversations, their observations, and those incidents that just happened spontaneously. Not a day went by without at least one gem worth recording. There's a LOL book out there waiting to be written.

LEADING FOURTH GRADERS

One day after eating lunch with the fourth graders in the school cafeteria, it was time for their class to line up quietly and walk single file back to the classroom, accompanied by their teacher. Ms. Cowan's class was ready to go and waiting for Ms. Cowan, who was running late. I was standing with the class when Chris, at the head of the line, turned to the cafeteria manager and inquired, "Can Karl take us back to our room?" The manager looked at me and considered the request with the proper concern, but before she could render a decision, Chris offered further support for his suggestion. "You don't have to worry. He's old enough." The cafeteria manager only laughed, patted me on the shoulder, and sent us down the long hallway.

AN ASTUTE OBSERVATION

I'd fallen during my evening walk and badly scraped my knee. The next day I was scheduled to volunteer in the fourth grade classroom. It was a warm fall day so I wore shorts, which exposed the minor injury to the class. Nine-year-old Ava stared intently at the scraped knee and finally inquired, "Karl, what did you do to your knee?" I assured her it was really nothing to worry about and explained how I had tripped on a sidewalk curb resulting in the minor scrape. Ava shook her head from side-to-side, rolled her eyes, and offered, "That's what happens when people get old."

REACHING MY GREAT- GRANDFATHER

While working with the third grade class on a project that involved U.S. postage stamps, I asked the kids to identify someone special to whom they would be sending a greeting card during the holiday season. All hands were raised immediately. The answers ranged widely. One said, "To my friend who lives across the street." Another said, "To my uncle who's serving overseas in the military." After patiently waiting her turn, another told the class, "My great-grandfather died just before Christmas last year. I didn't have his address so I mailed his card to God. That way I was sure he would get it."

KARL'S HERE!

I'm not sure who initiated it, but the students always greeted me with a chorus of "Karl's here!" when I entered the classroom. Ms. Canner shared a story with me from a teacher's aide. Apparently, when the students were coming in from recess one day, the aide asked Nat, one of Ms. Canner's students, "Nat, who is that person the kids always greet with 'Karl's here!' when he arrives at school?" "What?" said Nat. "You don't know Karl? He's da man, man."

JUNIOR JESUS . . .

In 2013 I compiled and published Just Call Me Junior Jesus . . . Words of Wisdom from Kids. It's a collection of short stories submitted by readers of Grammie Rules including humorous comments and observations by kids. Several stories came from school teachers – there certainly are more, many more to come! Not a day of volunteering went by without at least one unexpected comment by a student that made me smile.

STORY # 17 — WHAT THE TEACHERS SAY
∞ ∞ ∞

The following comments on volunteers in the classroom are from "my" two BES teachers and a good friend who recently retired after a 35-year elementary school teaching career.

Ms. Canner, Third Grade Teacher

Having another adult come into the classroom not only offers an extra pair of hands, but more importantly, another person that the kids can look up to. Each child has so many needs that require attention, it is impossible to meet them all. Another adult in the classroom who can offer guidance, education, and compassion is a huge help for the teacher and the students. Children need to know that there are adults who care and look out for them, and want to push them to be their very best. A good volunteer helps do that and more.

It's a real gift to see someone like Karl come into the classroom, give the kids an opportunity to have some fun, and someone to look up to. At times I feel so consumed by the teaching demands that I'd rather get my "classroom fix" as a volunteer than as a teacher. Karl made my day a bit easier and a lot more fun.

For the students, Karl became a mentor, a teacher, and a friend; for some, an "adopted" grandpa. He gave them a role model to have in their lives. Karl brought fun with him and made 18 lives better!

Ms. Cowan, Fourth Grade Teacher

Parent volunteers are a huge asset in my classroom. They help photocopy and laminate, organize and chaperone, read with the children, and even send in boxes of tissues and rolls of paper towels. Parent volunteers bring teachers coffee and help with many mundane tasks that teachers otherwise need to complete during their 20-minute lunch breaks, between meetings, or after school. By performing many tasks, these volunteers increase the time a teacher has to spend on class work with the students. Volunteers are lifesavers for teachers.

This year, however, I learned about a different type of volunteer: *the grandparent!* Karl walks into the classroom with a pocket full of peppermints, a box of freshly baked Munchkins, and beautiful cut flowers from his garden. Kids jump from their seats to greet him with a big hug and high fives, and never fail to announce, **"Karl's here!"**

Karl is a special volunteer like no other. He shares wisdom-rich stories, creates and plays math games with the kids, helps students become stronger writers, and even helps them realize that they are each authors. He has the gift of finding students' strengths and boosting their self-esteem. Karl makes school more fun for our students.

My Friend Cheryl, Retired Elementary School Teacher

I loved having volunteers in the classroom. Their contributions were amazing for both the students and the teacher. I was fortunate to have parent volunteers who had a genuine interest in the children. Their roles varied and all were important.

- Volunteers were always that extra pair of hands to help the students who needed more attention. These students always looked forward to the volunteer's return.
- Volunteers worked with individual students or a reading group to listen and help them read.
- I sought volunteers who wanted to share their hobbies/expertise with the students. The kids loved a change in the schedule/daily routine. Often the students continued to read about and research an interesting topic introduced by the volunteer.
- Special events during the school year could not have run smoothly without volunteer help: art projects, crafts festivals, plays, and poetry readings.
- Volunteers provided great one-on-one assistance to students in all subjects: math, social studies, writing, and science.

STORY # 18 — WHAT THE KIDS SAY
∞ ∞ ∞

Although volunteers are helpful to the teachers, the *real* recipients of a volunteer's efforts are the kids. There's no scientific way to measure a volunteer's contributions. But I enjoyed the third graders' written comments on my participation in their classroom, and the comments by the fourth graders on how volunteers helped in their classroom. I was pleased that many of the comments from both classes related to specific learning and fun experiences.

Ms. Canner had the third graders each write me a thank you letter (with art work) for my volunteer participation. She bound the letters into a booklet which they entitled **"Karl is the Best! Over a Hundred Reasons Why Karl is the Best Classroom Volunteer on Earth!"** Complete with class pictures, the booklet was presented to me at a special year-end class ice cream party.

From the third graders:

- Thank you Karl for sharing adventures with us and helping us.
- Thank you for making my dream of becoming an author come true.
- You also do a lot of things for us like read Scholastic News.
- You're the best grandfather volunteer ever in my opinion.
- I liked writing "Five Things That Matter."
- When you read us **Grammie Rules** I couldn't stop laughing.
- Thank you for all the books you brought us.
- Thank you for helping with our state project.
- I wish school could go into summer so we could spend more time with you.
- You have been a really good helper.
- The rock from Red Rock Canyon was amazing.
- Thank you for making this year more fun than school is supposed to be.
- Our field trips were great because you went along.
- Thank you for helping me with math.
- 7 times 5 plus 5 minus 10 times 10 times 5 = 1,500.
- I love learning about stamps.

Ms. Cowan asked her fourth graders to reflect on the school year and write comments on *how volunteers helped them and their class* during the year.

From the fourth graders:

- Helped us with our reading and math.
- Played learning games with us.
- Helped us with projects like our state map.
- Karl shared stories about his experiences.
- Helped Ms. Cowan organize, sort and file papers and books.
- Read to us and with us.
- Volunteers step in to help when the teacher is too busy.
- Volunteers are the best elderly in the world.
- Karl helped us become authors.
- Brought us great books for our classroom library.
- Joined us on field trips.
- Volunteers are golden.
- Volunteers save the teacher time so she can help us.
- Volunteers put smiles on kids faces.
- Brings great snacks.
- Played new games with us, like "Math Master."
- Helped us do new things like publish a book!
- Karl is awesome. Helped me learn math.
- We published our books and everyone got to write in it.

BY ELLA, A FOURTH GRADER

One day back in September, Ms. Cowan announced that Karl would be coming in. I didn't know who Karl was, but then Ms. Cowan said "Karl is Aidan's grandfather." When he finally came in, everyone said "Hi, Karl." He said "Hi, guys" to everyone. Weeks later we got used to Karl and greeted him whenever he walked in. Actually, I didn't, as I was shy. I don't know why. Finally, I talked with Karl and we became friends.

STORY # 19 — REFLECTIONS OF A SCHOOL VOLUNTEER
∞ ∞ ∞

Random thoughts as I reflect on my two-year volunteer experience with the third and fourth graders.

FUN. On every visit I tried to show the kids that I enjoyed coming to their classroom – and that *they* were the reason. We did have fun supporting the claim of many teachers that learning is easier when you're having fun in the process.

THEIR FAMILIES. The kids will make comments to you about their personal lives and usually they do expect a response. "I live with my mom because my dad lives in Georgia." "I get to see my mom this weekend." The volunteer is the adult and needs to be prepared to make an appropriate response. I never completely ended the conversation. Rather, I allowed the student to finish his/her thought and looked for a positive comment on their personal relationships.

LANGUAGE. All kids enjoy a little humor and one-on-one interaction. However, different kids will react differently when you respond to their comments. Finding each child's comfort level is important. With some kids I'd say, "Are you kidding me?" "Whatever!" "Really!" Others are more sensitive and your comments need to take a different tone. Learn your audience.

GIFTS. Gifts are welcomed and needed. Each teacher has a wish list of needed items, including notebooks, pencils, paper towels, hand cleaner, Kleenex, and more. With teacher approval, Dunkin' Donuts Munchkins were always popular.

THE TEACHER. Follow the teacher's lead. Students respect their teacher and wait for the teacher's direction. The volunteer needs to do the same.

BE PREPARED. *Question:* How long does it take a third or fourth grader to recognize that a volunteer has:

- Missed a spot shaving?
- Scraped a knee?
- A sty in his eye?
- New glasses?
- A new shirt?
- Gotten a haircut?
- A band-aid on a finger?
- Dirty fingernails from gardening?

Answer: 30 seconds or less.

A SAFE OUT. When a student asked about switching to a different activity or deviating from the plan, I usually took the safe way out. My answer: "We need to check with the teacher."

DISCIPLINE. Volunteers don't give yellow cards (two lead to a red card which leads to a note home!) or put a student in the "Chatterbox." My strongest discipline was: "Hey guys, come on. We can do better." Or simply, "Hey, cool it."

PARTICIPATION. I often joined the kids on the classroom rug for discussions and readings. I participated in their teacher-led math and word games, and in Q & A sessions on class work. I frequently raised my hand, hoping to be recognized. When the teacher was looking for silence her cues were "Clap, clap, clap-clap-clap." "Shhu, Shhhu, Shhuh- Shhuh-Shhuh." "Give me five." "Freeze, fourth graders." I always joined in. The kids love when the volunteer participates directly and becomes one of them.

BE PREPARED. The questions never end.

- May I go to the bathroom?
- How old are you?
- Did you go to school?
- Did you have Ms. Canner for a teacher?

- What is your wife's name?
- May I go to the bathroom?
- How often do you shave?
- Can you drive?
- Are you rich?
- Do you smoke?
- May I get a drink?
- Do you recycle?
- Do you have kids? Grandkids?
- May I go to the bathroom?

DISRUPTION. The kids will gravitate to the volunteer. When a student is engaged with a volunteer, suddenly three or four more students join the conversation, forcing the teacher to inquire: "Is everyone on task?" When students pursue the volunteer's attention, recognize that it might disrupt the class.

CLASSROOM CONTRIBUTIONS. There are many opportunities to bring items to the classroom to be used with study units and class activities. When I started to volunteer, I was wrapping up a four-year project to dispose of my own 3,000 book library. Chosen carefully to appeal, the new and different books were popular with the kids. I would often bring in books related to a subject on which they were working – for example, animals, space, or states. I'd make brief comments about the book and, if time permitted, even read a few pages to the class. Most learning games are popular and helpful additions to the classroom.

PRENUPTIAL AGREEMENT. The teacher's perceptions of a volunteer's role and the volunteer's perceptions might be quite similar or quite different. Ms. Canner and Ms. Cowan and I were on the same wave length regarding my role. The teacher and a new volunteer need a frank discussion about that volunteer's role. A clear understanding helps the volunteer fit into the teacher's overall teaching plan, and allows the volunteer opportunities to tailor his/her creativity and unique contributions to the classroom.

ENGAGING THE STUDENTS. There are many opportunities *(within limits)* for the volunteer to direct the class in activities at the teacher's expense.

Example 1. I wrote a silly poem entitled "Our School Mom" with individual reading parts and a joint class refrain. We "excused" Ms. Canner from the room for a short period on the Friday before Mother's Day to rehearse the reading. Upon her return, the class read "Our School Mom" and gave Ms. Canner a "School Mom" present.

Example 2. Before Ms. Cowan left the room briefly before the end of the day, she told the class, "Begin to get ready to leave. Karl's in charge." "Fun time?" I asked the kids. The kids' response was an enthusiastic "Yes!" I suggested we all become mimes and freeze in a position before Ms. Cowan returns. There they were, standing on one leg, lying on the floor, standing with arms outstretched, etc. Twenty-one motionless bodies (including Karl) waiting silently when Ms. Cowan walked in. They even showed little interest in the approaching dismissal time! Ms. Cowan could only smile and comment aloud, "This has to be the most well-behaved class I've ever had."

DRESS CODE. Most retirees relish the freedom from a workplace dress code. No more uniform, shirt and tie, business suit, and dress requirements. Those who enjoy a more casual dress code will be pleased to know it's usually the option for the school volunteer, at least in the elementary school situation. Volunteers should follow the teachers lead – casual and comfortable dress. Comfort and ease of movement is a priority when you spend eight hours with 20 nine-year-olds!

INITIATIVE. A volunteer quickly recognizes when he/she can take the initiative to help a student or a small group with an assignment. Doing so supports the busy teacher and the extra attention is welcomed by the students. Volunteers can play this role by becoming familiar with the individual kids, a familiarity that comes by observing students as they do class work. In some cases I would check with the teacher to express my interest in helping a particular student.

CHAOS AND ORDER. There is a fine line between chaos and

order in a third and fourth grade classroom. It goes with the territory, I guess, and at times a bit of fun comes with it. For the teacher it is a balancing act of allowing kids to be 8- and 9-year-olds, while having procedures and rules that are necessary to create a desirable learning environment. The best laid plans and instructions, explained in great detail at least three different ways, will still lead to questions. "What if...?" "Do you mean...?" "But should we follow...?" and "Can we...?" Patience. *And more patience.* As a volunteer I listened carefully to the teacher's instructions, hoping to keep one step ahead of the kids when asked the inevitable question, "What do I do now?"

MS. CANNER AND MS. COWAN. I would frequently share "school stories" with friends. I always referred to my teachers as "Ms. Canner" and "Ms. Cowan." A friend had an interesting observation, and a question. "I like your stories," he lied. "But why do you always talk about a 'Ms. Canner' or a 'Ms. Cowan?' Don't they have first names?" I sheepishly replied, "I guess so. But like the students, I've never used them.

OUTSIDE THE CLASSROOM

You will encounter the students and their parents at non-school activities. It's fun to see the students in a different setting, and interesting to introduce yourself and chat with their parents. Be prepared for anything. The most frequent parent response when meeting for the first time: "So . . . *you're* Karl!" I quickly focused on how much I enjoyed working with their child! Fortunately, they responded that their child's feeling was mutual. One mother told me that she knew when I had been to the classroom because her daughter's report on the day would begin with "Karl was in our class today and . . . . " When parents would mention a project on which I helped and the satisfaction their child expressed in doing the project – that was rewarding.

STORY # 20 — WHAT KEPT ME VOLUNTEERING
∞ ∞ ∞

The Kids – Fun

The kids themselves made every classroom visit fun. The behavior, candid comments and stories, and observations of third and fourth graders will do that. During every visit there were so many reasons to smile, to roll my eyes and shake my head. It was a pleasure to observe the interaction between kids, hear their laughter at a humorous story or classroom episode, hear their concern for the well-being of a classmate who went home sick, observe their inquisitive nature, and their genuine interest in helping each other.

The Kids – Learning

I helped a student who struggled with math and she finally said to me, "I got it. I can do it!" One boy told me, "I don't like to write." Then a week later he surprised me with a three-page story he had written and illustrated. "Karl, writing fiction is fun," he said. "Will you read my story?" There was daily personal satisfaction in aiding these students engage in learning and then watching them proudly display their new skill and what they had achieved. How could you not want to keep coming back?

The Teachers

I didn't select either Ms. Canner or Ms. Cowan to be my teachers for the volunteering experience. I simply followed my grandson Aidan to his assigned class. Would the experience have been different with other teachers? I don't know. What I do know is that both assignments worked for me. It worked because both teachers embraced the idea of a class volunteer. They gave me a chance to play multiple volunteer roles and bring my interests and life experiences to the classroom. They afforded me the opportunity to be a part of their teaching effort. This comment confirmed that I was part of the team: "If you have questions, raise your hand and either Karl or I will help." Oh, and they both had a quality that is mandatory for an elementary school teacher – a sense of humor.

A Learning Experience

School volunteering was a significant learning experience for me. For many reasons, school structure and approaches to teaching are constantly evolving. I learned about 21st century school schedules, priority given to student safety, and the important role that teachers' aides, special education teachers, and guidance counselors play. I observed firsthand how teachers and the support staff work with students who have diverse backgrounds, interests, and abilities. Their team effort to offer each student a successful learning experience was impressive.

Because I Could

Well, the idea of school volunteering was added to my retirement "to do" list after visiting the school with my grandson Aidan. And, I had the spare time. I kept returning because at the end of each day I believed I had accomplished something positive with at least one or more students. And, we had fun together. Is there another occupation where you can leave the work place every day with that feeling?

Made in the USA
Las Vegas, NV
15 April 2022

47556573R00035